THE LORD JESUS CHRSIT IS MY BRIDGE OVER TROUBLED WATERS

THE LORD JESUS CHRSIT IS MY BRIDGE OVER TROUBLED WATERS

DONALD THOMAS MAN OF FAITH

BMcTALKS Press
4980 South Alma School Road
Suite 2-493
Chandler, Arizona 85248

Copyright © 2020 by Donald Thomas. All rights reserved.

No part of this publication may be reproduced, stored in a retrieval system, or transmitted in any form or by any means, electronic, mechanical, photocopying, recording, scanning, or otherwise without the prior written permission of the Publisher. Requests to the Publisher for permissions should be submitted to the Permissions Department, BMcTALKS Press, 4980 S. Alma School Road, Ste 2-493, Chandler, AZ 85248 or at www.bmctalkspress.com/permissions

The views expressed in this publication are those of the author; are the responsibility of the author; and do not necessarily reflect or represent the views of BMcTALKS Press, its owner, or its contractors.

Volume pricing is available to bulk orders placed by corporations, associations, and others. For details, please contact BMcTALKS Press at info@bmtpress.com

FIRST EDITION

Library of Congress Control Number: 2020909609

ISBN: 978-0-9998901-9-6

TABLE OF CONTENTS

A Letter to the Reader   vii

1. When I Knew That God's Hand Was on My Life   11
2. The House of the Neighborhood and Family Loss   15
3. Sometimes Younger Brothers Follow Older Brothers   21
4. The Second Time God Used Me to Help Someone   25
5. I Found My Purpose in Life   29
6. Never Doubt What God Can Do for You   33
7. I Only Had the Lord   43
8. No One in Selma Knew   49
9. There is Good News to This Story   53
10. It's Going to Make You More of a Christian   61
11. It's Not Me Who is Doing Any of This   67
12. Satan Knocked Me Down But God Lifted Me Up!   75

A LETTER TO THE READER

My name is Donald Thomas. I would like to tell you a little story about my life. I was born in Selma, Alabama. No name was originally listed on my birth certificate because of a tragedy that occurred while my mother was in labor with me. "No Name Thomas" appeared on my birth certificate. Later, I had to actually give myself a name. Please continue reading, and I will describe more details of my life.

If you would like to read my first book, it's entitled *Donald Thomas, Man of Faith*. This book describes how the Lord took care of me during an attack on my life while I was in California in 1987. I was left for dead. I had broken jaws, blindness, paralysis, a caved-in chest, brain damage, and other life-threatening injuries. My first book tells how the Lord brought me through these harrowing times. This current book is concerning how the Lord has blessed me in many more ways.

1

WHEN I KNEW THAT GOD'S HAND WAS ON MY LIFE

To reiterate a story in my first book, I'll share with you one of the first major times I was aware of God's hand on my life, although I'm sure there were many other times. When I was only seven or eight years old, some new neighbors moved in nearby. I would often sneak away with them to the creek to go swimming. My mother would warn me against this.

One day, I had slipped away from home with about five of these neighbor friends. We went to an old school; there was a creek located just behind the school. There was also a muscadine tree. Because we were only children, we didn't pay attention to the posted signs at the creek, which warned "Do not swim in this creek." The signs were posted because there were sinkholes in this creek.

One of the older kids climbed the tree and started shaking the muscadines out of the tree. The muscadines fell into the creek, and we jumped in and tried to catch them. After I jumped into the water, I felt something begin to pull me around and around. The swirling motion pulled me under the water. I had no control and was unable to pull myself from under the water. I felt sticks and rocks hitting my legs. The sinkhole continued to pull me farther down.

Suddenly, the Lord pulled me away from this massive, strong force of the sinkhole, and I was able to swim to the bank of the creek. As I climbed out of the water, I saw two long, green snakes swimming in the water in just about the location where I had jumped in. The Lord had pulled me out just in time. Someone who had seen us headed to the creek came and checked on us. This is just one example of how the Lord has blessed me in my life. He spared my life that day.

2

THE HOUSE OF THE NEIGHBORHOOD AND FAMILY LOSS

THE LORD JESUS CHRIST IS MY BRIDGE OVER TROUBLED WATERS

I grew up playing basketball in the backyard of my mother and father's home. I would play basketball until I could play no longer because I was so tired. I played on the weekends from sunup until sundown. I became talented in playing the game of basketball. Our house was the "house of the neighborhood" because we simply played "clean" fun. There was no fighting, no drugs, and no alcohol. Some great basketball players originated from this backyard. Many hours were spent there playing because we enjoyed the game and the get-together so much.

I lived across the street from a noisy café. A lot of violence happened at this café. A lot of shooting and stabbing events took place on the weekends. I wanted to be able to leave this neighborhood. I didn't want my family or myself to continue to live in this violent and dangerous neighborhood, so I played basketball to the best of my ability to hopefully be able to win a scholarship, go to college, and further my education. I wanted to become a professional basketball player.

However, while I was growing up, there were many distractions in my life. One of my brothers, who was only eight years old at the time, passed away while my mother was in labor with me. We almost lost my mother too during this time. She had a difficult time in labor with me after hearing the horrible news of my brother's death. I was a large baby, weighing somewhere between twelve and thirteen pounds. There were several children in my family; two babies died in childbirth. All this stress also seemed to affect my life.

We were all a close family and loved one another. Some of my siblings are so much older than me that they could actually pass for my mother or my father. My oldest brother is twenty years older than me. My older sister is thirteen years older than me.

I lost my wonderful mother in 2016. This was a great loss in our lives. I thank the Lord that she is with Him now, and He is taking care of her. I have confidence in her and faith in God. I would like to mention that I'm still here on Earth because of God's goodness. He brought me through a wide valley and I'm grateful to Him. I'm thankful for what God has done for me in my life.

When I was about ten years old, my thirteen-year-old brother and I went to Tennessee to visit an older brother. We stayed for a portion of the summer for a three- or four-week visit. We had a really nice time. We had a lot of fun playing basketball together in my older brother's backyard. He did a good job taking care of us. Some of his neighbors joined us for the games.

The day came that we had to cut short our visit because we learned that another brother had arrived in Alabama from California. We wanted to see him. We were much more familiar with our brother who lived in Tennessee than the brother who lived in California because we saw him more often when he would visit our home. The brother who lived in California had left home when we were young. When we arrived back home from Tennessee, we met our brother and his wife and two children. We were really glad to see him. We thanked God for this opportunity. My mother was also thrilled to see her son from California.

When my brother from California arrived in Alabama, we wanted to be with him all the time because we were so glad to see him. We were also glad to be able to get to know him. He would take us riding around to places that we had never seen as children. Neither my mother nor my father was a driver during my childhood years; we normally walked around the neighborhood to explore. So riding with my brother was a really big treat. My older brother enjoyed taking one of my brothers and me to the YMCA so we could attend swimming classes. Later, these swimming lessons proved to be a blessing.

3

SOMETIMES YOUNGER BROTHERS FOLLOW OLDER BROTHERS

This book focuses on how the Lord instilled in me at a young age the ability to help others, so I'd like to share with you the first time God used me. This story has been "inside" me for a long while; I've never told this story. However, recently, while talking with my wife, I felt as though the Lord would have me share this story to show His glory.

The first time God used me and gave me the ability to help someone was one day when my brother and several family members decided to go to Valley Creek Lake at Paul M. Grist State Park to swim and barbeque. This was located in Selma, Alabama. My brother cooked fish by wrapping them in tinfoil and placing them on the grill.

My brother who had gone to Tennessee with me was three years older. We were all having a good time at the lake, playing music, and enjoying other activities. This brother wandered off, all the way over to the other side of the lake, where there was a diving board at the edge of the lake and the water was deeper. No one really paid attention enough to see that he had wandered away. The Lord led me to look up to see my brother leaving, going away from all of us. I don't know if the Lord was leading me there with my brother or if I was just simply following him. Sometimes younger brothers follow older brothers.

I didn't know that I was going to save his life. I felt led to run as fast as I could to catch up to my brother. When I caught up to him, he was already diving off the diving board. He probably didn't realize how deep the water was in that area. When he hit the water, he started yelling for help, saying he was drowning. He was panicking and splashing around in the water. He couldn't get out. Because I was so young, I didn't know what to do. I felt led to jump into the water to save my brother's life. It did not occur to me that I was not an experienced enough swimmer to save him.

My brother was bigger than I was. He was splashing so much from fear that I had to struggle with him. He almost drowned me with the splashing and reaching. I held him by his waist and was able to pull him safely to the shore. I never told my mother or my other siblings. I didn't think it was a really big deal. However, as I've thought about it later, this story truly shows the power of God.

4

THE SECOND TIME GOD USED ME TO HELP SOMEONE

The second time God used me to help someone concerns my mother. One day, she was frying bacon on the stove. At the same time, she was also getting my younger sister dressed for school. Our house was small. There were at least five children home at that time. The other siblings had already left home. While she was distracted and helping my sister get dressed, the bacon and the grease became extremely hot.

When I entered the room, I saw the iron skillet was starting to smoke, and then a flame followed. The fire was about to travel up the wall. I ran over to the stove and picked up the skillet so that I could quickly place it in the sink and fill it with water. During this process, however, because the skillet was so heavy and I was so young and small, the grease in the skillet that had become hot enough to turn into a blazing fire spilled from the side of the skillet onto my fingers. I ran cold water over my fingers. Although my fingers were badly burned, I was able to save our house from burning that day.

Later, when I was outside playing with the other children, I was in much pain from the burn. I ran back and forth, running water over my fingers. My fingers were burned. My mother saw me, stopped me, and asked me why I was doing this. Then I had to tell her that I had been burned by trying to put out a fire in the skillet. My mother said she was proud I had done this, and that I had saved our home. "Thank you for it, son. You are a good son, but I hate that you burned your fingers. I'm going to get something to put on it because I see blisters."

My mother poured hydrogen peroxide over my fingers and then comforted me the rest of the time. She made sure I had everything I needed and showed me a lot of care. She thanked me again because we were a low-income family and could not have afforded to have our house burn or to buy another house.

5

I FOUND MY PURPOSE IN LIFE

Because this is a story to share with you about how the Lord instilled a gift in me to help others, I'll share with you yet another story about how God helped me to help my other brother when I traveled to California. I was staying at my brother's house. My brother and his wife had planned an evening of romance. They were going to sit in the living room and light the logs in the fireplace. However, my brother placed gasoline on the wood in the fireplace and threw a match into the fireplace.

A fire started blazing. He panicked. I was in the dining room while all this was happening. Suddenly, I heard a commotion; my sister-in-law was screaming. My brother was yelling, "I've got to put this fire out!" The fire had spread out of the confines of the fireplace and was moving toward the sofa and the curtains.

I did what the Lord directed me to do. I grabbed a blanket and began trying to put out the fire. I continued to smother the fire with the blanket, beating the flames until the fire went out. That's how the Lord blessed me to be able to save my brother's beautiful home in California. I thank God for using me, even still today.

I've looked over what God has had me do in my life. He inspired me to write my first book, which told what God had used me to do. The intention was to show people the goodness of God. God is still as alive today as He was in the time of Moses, Abraham, Elijah, Joshua, and Samson. He is still doing miraculous things.

I would like for this book to be a help to others, to show that the Lord has used me to help others, and to also share how He has helped me. I found out that is my purpose in life—not just to look out for myself but to look out for my fellow man and woman. So what I've done is my purpose. I'm writing these books because that is what God inspired me to do. The stories in these books are true stories, like the story I just shared with you about an eight- or nine-year-old child, diving into a dangerous and deep lake for the love of his brother, not caring and not knowing what he was really going to do, risking his own life. What was on my mind was saving my brother's life.

It was the grace of God that my mother didn't have to bury two children; we both could have drowned. I'd had only a couple of swimming lessons and did not swim that well. I am 57 years old now. My brother I saved is sixty years old. I haven't really talked about this story until now. I wasn't inspired to do so until now.

6

NEVER DOUBT WHAT GOD CAN DO FOR YOU

In a continuation of my "calling" from God to help others, I would also like to help people who have post-traumatic stress disorder. This condition is a dangerous health problem. Many times, it affects those who have fought in a war, but it is not always limited to their situations. I have personal knowledge of this condition because I was diagnosed with it after experiencing a horrific experience in my own life.

There was a time in my life when I had moved to California and was living and working there. I was the supervisor over the junior clerks in a grocery store. I worked at several different grocery stores in California, even the largest one in the world. I really enjoyed working there. I loved what I was doing.

My job was to prevent any accidents in the store—to keep all items off the floor like water; grease; or anything slippery that might cause customers to slip, fall, and hurt themselves. This, of course, was meant to decrease lawsuits. I don't recall anyone falling in the store while I worked there. I had some dependable guys who worked under my supervision. We worked well together. I never really had a problem with any of them. Everyone came to work and knew what their jobs were and completed their responsibilities.

One night, on June 18, 1987, I was on my way home from work. I normally rode the bus to about three blocks away from where I lived in Lynwood, California. As I was crossing the street, I was suddenly brutally attacked from behind by a gang. When they hit the back of my head, I fell face first onto the pavement on the street. The criminals continued to kick me and beat me in my side, my stomach, my legs, and my back. They beat me with all their might while I lay on the ground. I passed out from the harsh blows to my head. They left me in the dark street.

I was left in the street for dead for over eight hours. Then, I was taken to the trauma department at Martin Luther King, Jr. Community Hospital. I had been gravely injured. These blows injured me so badly that I was considered to be nonexistent. I was hit in the head several times, which resulted in a concussion. I was kicked so hard that it broke my jaws. I was also left paralyzed and blind from this attack.

I am thankful to this day that God used this hospital to save my life. The medical staff gave me many shots because they expected my pain to be so severe. They asked me if I wanted "twilight sleep." I was told the shots themselves could have killed me in my fragile condition. I was afraid to sleep, so I declined their offer of the twilight sleep. I felt if I went to sleep, that I would not wake up again. I was unable to correctly talk because my jaws were hanging with nothing attached. I couldn't close my mouth. I couldn't see for the blood running down from my skull. This blood caused my eyes to become infected, which in turn caused the blindness. I couldn't walk or move. However, the Lord blessed me.

I did not have any medical benefits that would help me, so after staying at the hospital a while, I was prematurely checked out by a family member. This family member promised to take me to my follow-up appointments but failed to do so. The family member was supposed to be responsible for taking me to my appointments and also for taking care of me. It was another family member who finally admitted this. The name was also on the hospital records. Today, this would be called neglect.

I was left alone and had no type of medical home health assistance. I had to just depend on the Lord for everything. My mouth was wired together, so I was unable to eat correctly. I was unable to see. The doctor wrote a prescription for the pain, but not one pill was given to me. So, you see, God really blessed me during this time. I was paralyzed for almost a year. This is a reminder that nothing is impossible for the Lord Jesus Christ to do.

As I mentioned, I did not have proper care after my dismissal from the hospital. My mouth was wired shut because of the broken jaws; I couldn't eat anything solid. I was tortured after the attack because people would enjoy eating things like barbeque around me because they knew I couldn't eat. Barbeque has an intense aroma, so smelling it made me want to eat it.

When someone who hasn't eaten real food in a long time smells the aroma of grilled meat, like ribs or chicken, it can really bother them. It can make them do something that will hurt themselves just to be able to get a piece of the food. No one seemed to care. Instead of trying to help me, they tortured me. It probably would have killed me to try to eat because I would have had to jerk the wires from my mouth.

After about a year of having my mouth wired tightly shut, I was about to try to remove the wires when the doctor from Martin Luther King, Jr. Community Hospital in Los Angeles called me. I had smelled the scent of the grilled food coming inside my apartment, and I was really hungry. I felt as though I was screaming to myself, "Somebody, help me. Help me!" I was thinking, "Dear Lord, help me."

Then the Lord had the phone ring. The doctor said, "Mr. Thomas, the reason I'm calling you is because it's time to take the wires out of your mouth. We want you to come to the hospital today and get the wires out." God had recently made it possible for me to begin walking and seeing again. So I got up, but my legs were still weak. Sometimes they felt like rubber.

God had told me to come out of the apartment, and that He was going to heal me and make me a great person, "a living testimony of what I can do for you." Never doubt what God can do for you. He continued, "Even to the people who were responsible for your injuries, I'm going to show what your God can do for you." So God had me "come forward" out of the apartment. When He told me that, I obeyed Him.

I got up and walked out of the apartment. When I left, my family, who was sitting outside grilling, looked at me like they had seen a ghost. They didn't believe I was ever going to come out of the apartment alive. None of my relatives who were sitting in the yard grilling offered to even say, "How are you doing? Can I do anything for you? Can I give you a ride somewhere?"

As I walked, I was wobbling because my legs were weak, and I was off-balance. I was depending on the Lord to see me through. He put one leg in front of the other for me. I didn't know the way to the hospital. The Lord led me from Lynwood to Compton and on to Los Angeles. On the way to the hospital, my legs continued to feel weak, causing me to stagger. I went all the way from Lynwood to Compton.

When I got to Compton Boulevard, a gang fight was happening. The victim ran to the side of the street, but the gang members were terrorizing him. They were swinging bricks and sticks at another guy who was running from the gang. They were intending to kill him. Beer bottles and bricks were flying over my head as I was staggering down the street. The Lord did not let one piece of the flying items touch me. I just walked right through them. It was like walking through a storm. That was the goodness of my Lord Jesus Christ! The Lord was still holding my hand and guiding me to the hospital.

When I arrived at the hospital, a nice nurse came up to me and asked where I needed to go. I was tired and breathing hard. I mumbled to her and showed her my mouth. She lowered her head so she could hear me. I mumbled to her that the doctor had called me and told me to come get the wires removed. The Lord allowed her to understand what I was mumbling. So she led me straight to the trauma department.

There, the doctor immediately started removing the wires. As he worked, he told me that someone should have been taking me to my appointments because the wires had grown into my gums; this was a problematic situation. He informed me that he would need to give me several shots to deaden my mouth. It took over seventeen shots to deaden my mouth. The wires had not been adjusted the entire time since I had them inserted.

After I had the wires removed, I tried to get back to normal. I felt God urging me to get up and try to eat, talk, and walk. As I previously mentioned, I had no one to help me or take care of me during this time. I had no other way to pay my bills, to eat, or to take care of myself.

7

I ONLY HAD THE LORD

I tried to go back to work. I went to see my previous boss and told him that I was able to work again. He was glad to see that the Lord had blessed me to overcome all the life-threatening injuries I had received. He said he was proud of me to have gone through what I had experienced and that I was still trying to do things to help myself. I told him that I needed to start working right away because I had no money, food, or medicine; I only had the Lord.

He was a religious, kindhearted manager of the store in Los Angeles. He told me that I was a good worker and could start anytime I was ready. I told him that I would like to start the next day. He instructed me to come in the next day and use the work schedule I had used previously. I was to go to work about seven A.M. He placed me on light duty. Previously, I had worked 48 hours per week with one day off per week. That is what I began working again because that is what it took to pay my bills.

I was so hungry because I had not eaten. I went to one aisle in the store and took a bag of potato chips and ate them. The manager questioned me and said someone had seen me eating the chips. He told me not to do that anymore because other people would see me and that his boss would make him fire me. I told him I wouldn't do it anymore and I didn't. I tried to continue working but was unable to continue. I was about to learn why. There were other factors causing problems in my life. I was diagnosed with insomnia and post-traumatic stress disorder, which originated from the attack on my life.

I had never heard of these sicknesses. My condition became so severe that I was hospitalized. The night-shift nurse who was responsible for caring for me and was assigned to watch me during sleep noticed how fitfully I slept at night. I would sleep a little while and then wake up in a rage. The nurse said that due to my sleep patterns, I showed signs of post-traumatic stress disorder. The nurse asked me if I had ever been diagnosed with this condition.

This really alarmed me because I had never heard this term. I had heard the term "shell-shocked" as it related to military personnel who had experienced bombs and shooting. To calm my alarm about hearing this, the nurse said, "Mr. Thomas, I have post-traumatic stress disorder. I'm a veteran. I've been in the service." Because he was a nurse and working at the hospital, this made me feel somewhat better. He explained this sickness to me. He asked if I had ever been in a war, but I told him I had not. He asked me to tell him why I was in the hospital. It had been previously difficult for me to relate this story because it seemed as though it made me live the event over again in my mind.

I told him the story about how I had been attacked, robbed, beaten, and left for dead in California in 1987. I explained to him that I had been hit in my head. I was also diagnosed with insomnia. Because of this, I had tried to self-medicate by drinking alcohol to be able to sleep. Later, I was prescribed five or six medications for insomnia, and I still had trouble sleeping.

So I had to leave California and go back to my hometown of Selma, Alabama. I went to live with my mother. I was not able to function or continue to work. I couldn't take care of myself. Although I had two brothers and two sisters in California at that time, they were not doing anything to help me.

8

NO ONE IN SELMA KNEW

When I arrived in Alabama, I was thin due to not eating. I was probably about 120 pounds. When my mother first saw me, she was glad to see me and urged me to come in and get something to eat. She started feeding me from the time I arrived. I started gaining a little weight. I would eat anything she placed in front of me. No matter how much I ate, it seemed like I couldn't get full. She would cook everything she could pull from the refrigerator because she knew something was wrong with me. I didn't tell her what the problem was because I didn't want her to be upset.

When I had been injured the night of the attack, none of my siblings called home to let my other family know of the attack. They didn't tell my brothers or sisters, my aunts or uncles, or even my grandmother who was living at that time. So no one in Selma knew they were needed to help me. After I told my story to my mother and my grandmother, they said, "If we had known that you had been injured, we would have come to help you, even if we had to walk, rather than have you hurt with no one to help."

So none of my Alabama family members knew of my horrible time in California. I was in that situation for over a year, trying to recover from my injuries. The Lord was with me every step of the way. He held my hand. I really want you, the reader, to know of the goodness of the Lord. He held my hand through paralysis, He held my hand through blindness, and He held my hand through major brain damage. I would not have known this last diagnosis unless I had seen it on my hospital discharge paperwork. The brain damage was due to having been hit so many times in my head, even in the back of my head.

9

THERE IS GOOD NEWS TO THIS STORY

Then, as time went on, I met my wife, who continues to be a big inspiration in my life. I had actually met her the first time about a week or two before I left to go to California. My wife and I are happily married. We have three daughters and ten grandchildren. We are thankful to God for each other.

We were living in an apartment, and one day she shared with me that she would like to move to the country. She was sick at that time and felt as though she would feel better living in the country. My uncle had some land out in the country and had given me some of the land. I had not mentioned it to her because I had just received it shortly before I met her again. I told her that the Lord had blessed me with some land.

My uncle and his wife had always been good to me and to all my mother's children. When we were children, he and his wife would come pick us up and take us to the country to see his animals. He had a plantation with cows, white stallions, hogs, goats, dogs, and cats. This was exciting to us as children. His wife would make ice cream, cheese, and buttermilk. She would get her little stool and show us how to milk the cows. My uncle would show us how to smoke a hog and preserve it in the smokehouse. They would also show us about country baking, which was good! I'm thankful for my uncle.

When we got a little older, he would come get me and my two older brothers and we would help him put hay in the barn. This would be done at the end of summer, as the cows and horses would need something to eat during the cold wintertime. He showed us how to bale the hay, and we would stack it inside the barn. Then he would take us to get something to eat and take us back home. He would often visit us. Any time he thought he could help us or our mother, he would. He was really a great uncle.

All my family members on my mother's side were helpful. She had nine brothers and sisters—ten siblings total. Now, I don't have any aunts or uncles remaining; all of them have passed away. My mother was the youngest of the siblings and was a twin. She died in 2016. My father passed away when I was young. I only knew a few people on my dad's side of the family—a couple of cousins. So I only have my wife, my children, and my brothers and sisters left for my family. Many of my siblings have "gone their own way." I'm thankful for my family members.

My father was a great provider. My mother was a great homemaker. She did what she could to teach the children right from wrong. I can't speak for the others, but what she taught me is still in me. She taught us to always pray to God and thank Him and to do what is right. Don't let Satan try to turn us to doing wrong. Pray before you do things. Pray before you go to bed at night. Pray before you eat. She taught us to respect our elders. She taught us boys to respect the girls.

Due to the post-traumatic stress disorder, I had flashbacks of what had happened to me the night I was attacked. I could see myself lying in my own blood. These scenes flashed over and over in my mind. This was scary. Later, each time I had a flashback, or an episode of post-traumatic stress, it was hard for me to "come out of it."

While I would sleep, I would rest for only about fifteen minutes before I would wake up screaming and in a rage. My wife would gently attempt to bring me out of this state. The nurses had instructed her to quietly try to awaken me, not suddenly. I was then on eight powerful medications. Sometimes I still could not sleep. I was trying to work in Selma, but I was having a difficult time working the long hours. The employers saw that I was really trying to work to support my family, so sometimes they would ask me to work extra hours. I wouldn't turn it down, even though I was in pain.

While I was at work, my grandmother, whom I loved dearly, passed away at 95 years old. She lived a beautiful life. She had been the organist at her church for about fifty or sixty years. I have a musical family; they are talented singers and instrumentalists. She was a wonderful grandmother to me and all my siblings. She had always been good to my mother and my father; my father was her son.

My father was a genius. He was one of the first black men to repair televisions in our area. He was the only one at that time in Selma able to repair TVs. I used to watch my father work on the TVs. He would sometimes stay up at night working on them after working all day as a butcher at the grocery store.

I'm the youngest son of seven brothers of the family, and I'm the only one who took up the trade of butchering. I went to meat-cutting school in Selma when I first graduated from high school. This took nine months of training. I received a certificate for the best "boner" of the class. They were able to get me a job right away in a new supermarket that had just opened. I was about seventeen years old and had two children. However, I made a mistake when I was young; I missed work and didn't call in to let my boss know that I was not coming in. I lost this job.

To make a long story short, I returned from California and was working in a supermarket again when my grandmother passed. I had stayed at work late that day to help customers who might need help with something like slicing a ham for them in the way they preferred. I also stayed late on some particular days to clean the meat department. I was at work by myself, preparing the meat for the next day.

I received a phone call informing me that my grandmother had passed away. After I hung up the phone, I tried to begin working again. But after receiving this news, I had a flashback and cut three fingers on my right hand almost completely off. They were almost hanging. I didn't tell anyone at work about what happened because before the incident, I had never been cut at work.

The saws in the meat market were strong because they were sometimes used for cutting animal bones. I'm just blessed that it didn't cut off my entire hand. I was bleeding so badly that I wrapped my hand in a cloth. I was so out of it that I ran out of the meat department and went home. My wife saw my fingers and wanted me to go to the doctor, but I told her that it would be okay. It kept bothering me so much that I did finally go to the emergency room the next day.

The doctor said, "Your fingers need stitches, but I cannot put stitches in because the wounds have been open over sixteen hours." So the doctor was unable to use stitches. I called my boss and told him what had happened. He had seen the blood on the floor. He still wanted me to put a glove on my hand and come into work, which I did. I was placed on light duty. I wanted to do what I could to keep my job. After I returned to work, my post-traumatic stress disorder continued to worsen until I had to return to the hospital. The doctor then removed me from work.

The post-traumatic stress was causing more problems in my life than the night I was attacked. It was causing tremors. It was also causing additional stress to my brain, and I especially didn't need this because I already had brain damage from the attack. However, there is good news to this story. I'd like to discuss how the Lord helped me to keep the post-traumatic stress disorder in order.

10

IT'S GOING TO MAKE YOU MORE OF A CHRISTIAN

Post-traumatic stress was about to get the best of me. The medication was helping, but it was not curing me. Even though the disease had worsened, God began teaching me how to deal with this post-traumatic stress. The Lord began instructing me to write a book, but I felt as though I could not obey. I felt like Noah must have felt when God told him to build the ark. I even asked my wife if she could write it for me, but she declined. She said she had not experienced the events and it was something the Lord wanted me to do personally.

God continued to press on me to write a book, to tell what God had done for me and what He brought me through. I continued to wonder how to accomplish this task. God told me that He would provide all the tools I needed to write a book. So I stopped questioning the Lord and just accepted that it was something He wanted me to do. I had learned previously, when I was alone in my recovery, during all the painful times associated with blindness, paralysis, concussion, chest depressions, and broken ribs, that He was the only One I could trust. I concluded that I had to trust Him because He was the only One who had been there for me. If He told me to write a book and told me that He would give me what I needed, then that's what I would do.

God showed me that I was going to be healed without medication. I was to be healed by talking about my trauma and sharing it in my first book. God told me to write my book and be healed! He said, "It's going to make you feel better. It's going to make you get along with your wife better. It's going to make you more of a Christian. It's going to make you somebody because you are going to be able to be a living testimony of what I've brought you through."

I got some paper and started writing. I wrote more. God showed me how to do it better. He showed me who to get in touch with to type the book for me. He showed me who to contact for publishing the book. God continued to instruct me how to write my first book and share what I felt, what I had experienced, who I hated for doing this, what I disagreed with about it, and let the anger and rage emerge.

The Lord spoke to me again and said, "Donald, I want you to write this book because I want the world to know what I did for you. I've done for you what I did for other men, way before your time, back in the biblical days. What I've done for you is bring you from death."

So, I continued in my effort of doing what the Lord had asked me to do. He gave me what it took to write that first book, *Donald Thomas, Man of Faith*. My second book was titled *I Died and the Lord Jesus Christ Gave Me Life*

Again, Donald Thomas: A Man of Faith. When the book was completed and published, my pastor read the book and was so impressed that he placed a copy in Brown Chapel A.M.E. Church in Selma, Alabama. It was placed in the archives with other books like those about Dr. Martin Luther King, Jr.; former US President Barack Obama; and Rosa Parks.

11

IT'S NOT ME WHO IS DOING ANY OF THIS

After a long time of taking eight prescribed medications a day for the post-traumatic stress disorder, probably for close to 25 years, my wife noticed that I was sleeping a lot, even before taking my medicine at night and even sometimes during the day. She decided that she wanted to speak to my doctor about this, so she went with me to my doctor's appointment.

When she told the doctor that I had started sleeping without having to take medication, the doctor was surprised and knew that I must have had a breakthrough with insomnia. She was surprised because not many people overcome insomnia. That is another reason I'm thankful to God. He allowed me to overcome this terrible problem.

I now have only a few "bad" nights of sleep. Most of the time I sleep peacefully, and I thank God for this peaceful sleep. I thank God that He is working in my life. The doctor said that she would continue to prescribe the medication for insomnia but instructed me to only use it as I needed it. I'm thankful my wife noticed the change in my sleep patterns. This was a major problem the Lord worked out that originated from my injuries.

God used writing these books to heal me of this horrific disease. God wanted to help me overcome the flashbacks and associated post-traumatic stress that I had at the time. This was originating from rage, from anger about the attack. This disease was keeping me from living a normal life. It was preventing me from being comfortable. It was stopping me from sleeping. It was not allowing me to be happy and joyful like the Lord wanted me to be.

God wanted me to experience what He could do for me and to be able, through all these life-threatening injuries, to tell others what He did for me. He wanted me to always put my trust in Him. He wanted me to never doubt what He can do. He inspired me to write everything that was bothering me and put it into a story that would become a book. God told me that He wanted me to write everything that I experienced the night I was attacked. He said He would help me remember everything that happened that night.

After I began to tell my story, I started to feel better. I was able to skip my sleep medication. The flashbacks went away. I haven't had a flashback or an episode in over three years. I thank God for that. My wife can verify this as the truth. When I began to write, I began to sleep a peaceful sleep with no bad dreams, no waking often during the night. I was able to smile again. I no longer had to fear and dread having a flashback.

This touch of God in my life made me more of a Christian. Most important, I was able to speak and share what happened to me without having a flashback. It made me more of a believer in God. That's the purpose for this third book: to tell what He has done in my life and to share what God has instilled in me from childhood—to tell about a love for my brothers and sisters that God has placed in my heart.

Now, in this present book, I want to encourage others and show what great things the Lord's hands have done. I intend to help those the Lord leads me to help. Right now, I would like to help veterans and others who have suffered from post-traumatic stress disorder by telling them how the Lord helped me to overcome insomnia and to keep my post-traumatic stress disorder under control. As I previously stated, I haven't had an episode in over three years. I am proud to say that I feel much better. Before, when I would have an episode or flashback, it would leave a lasting effect for the next few days.

I thank God for touching my body. I also thank God for using people in my life to help me such as my wife for noticing the change in my sleep patterns and the medical staff of doctors and nurses for all their help. I thank God for my wife, my children, my friends, and my sponsors who helped with the first and second books.

God has reminded me, "I held your hand from the time you were injured. I held your hand when you were in a sinkhole. I held your hand when you jumped in the lake to save your brother. I've held your hand ever since you've been in this world."

When I wrote the book, I placed everything in the book that had been bothering me—things I was holding inside that were causing me to have flashbacks at night. Before, I had problems talking about this attack because of what I would experience after I talked about the attack. So when I talked about what happened the night of June 18, 1987, it would cause me to have a flashback, either then or later that night when I lay down to sleep. I was afraid of what the flashback would do to me.

My wife and I usually talk a lot, but it was a long time before she knew what happened to me because I didn't want to talk about it. That was highly unusual because we've always enjoyed talking and sharing experiences. Now, we try to enjoy our time together and take our minds off our problems. We also share what God has done in our lives and pray together. That's what's keeping us here today and keeping us going forward; we put our trust in God.

I have tried to help my family members who were having problems. I have tried to offer them advice and tell them what God has done for me. Many people who read my first book have shared with me that it was a great help to them. Some people even told me that they would have ended their lives, if they had not read the book. Some of their situations were due to relationship breakups.

People were inspired by what God had done for me, which gave them more willpower and inspiration that God would do the same for them. They saw how I had been through the storm and had been brought through the storm by God. They saw my life as a walking miracle given by God. It's not me who is doing any of this; it's God *through* me. I could not do *anything* without the help of the Lord.

12

SATAN KNOCKED ME DOWN BUT GOD LIFTED ME UP!

There are so many people who need help. I want to help these people. I want them to know that God is with me. If God was with me and held my hand through all that trouble, He can hold your hand. Like those who had thought of ending their lives because of a breakup in a relationship, God can put that relationship together again if it's right.

I would also like to offer special thanks to the counselors of Selma, Alabama and the mayor of Selma for their help with my book. The doctors who treated me, along with my wife, also deserve my gratitude. I also appreciate those who sponsored my books. The Lord helped me to overcome anger in my life, even to the point of marrying my wife. We enjoy life together and pray together. God brought pastors into our lives who presently share my book in radio commercials. All the rage and anger inside me had to be brought out in order to have complete healing. This rage was making me sicker and could have gotten to the point of causing me to do something I would regret. God changed all the negative into positive. He caused me to do something that I could be proud of—from now on.

I hope those who have similar problems with post-traumatic stress disorder and insomnia will read this book and be helped. God first removed the insomnia and then helped me control the post-traumatic stress disorder. God made the way!

I'm better able to communicate with people. I'm able to love again. God cleared the rage and anger from my heart, body, and soul over what had happened to me in California by giving me the knowledge and wisdom to write true books.

So to remind you, the reader, once again, God has always held my hand. Everyone should thank the Lord and praise Him. When a baby is born, someone needs to start thanking God for the child. If people can't get over something from the past, they can't continue in well-being in the future. That's what was keeping me from receiving the blessings of God. I couldn't get a complete signal from God with my mind cloudy with negative thoughts. The negative was placed in me from the attack. I felt as though I could never love.

God showed me another way. He showed me that He could instill peace and healing in me and change me. If it can change me, it can change you. It can change everybody. The injuries I experienced were not overcome in a night's time. Some of my injuries are probably injuries that most people don't survive. I am a survivor. Satan knocked me down, but God lifted me up!

I want to help bring joy to others. I want to help them to overcome what Satan is trying to do against them. Add up all the anger, add up all the rage, and put it into a book. Get that book published. Read your own book—your own testimony. It will make you feel better. This book tells of a happier occasion than my first book. Don't give up. Keep your faith in God. God will never leave us. We are the ones who left God. Again, He will never leave us.

Ask God to keep His hand in yours and to be that "fence" around you. This is the man of faith speaking, Donald Thomas. Thank you so kindly, and God bless you and be with you. Always keep God first!

POST A REVIEW

Please leave your feedback on reading this book.

1. Visit www.amazon.com
2. Type in the search field the book's title along with my last name, "Thomas"
3. Scroll down, and click on "Write a customer review"

Let me know what you thought of the book and what you gained from it.

I read every review. They are tremendously helpful! Thank you!

www.ingramcontent.com/pod-product-compliance
Lightning Source LLC
Chambersburg PA
CBHW050444010526
44118CB00013B/1680